Who Sniffs with This Nose?

by Cari Meister

PEBBLE
a capstone imprint

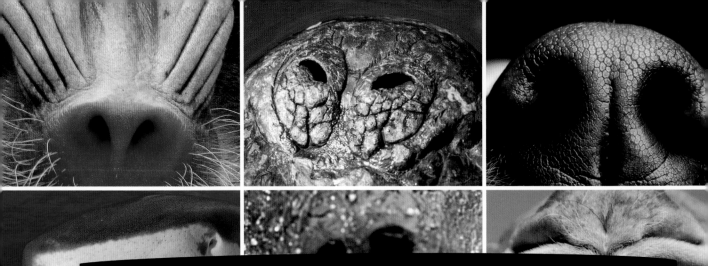

Animal noses come in all sorts of wonderful shapes, sizes, and colors. Who sniffs with this nose? Guess, then turn the page to find out!

Who sniffs with this nose?

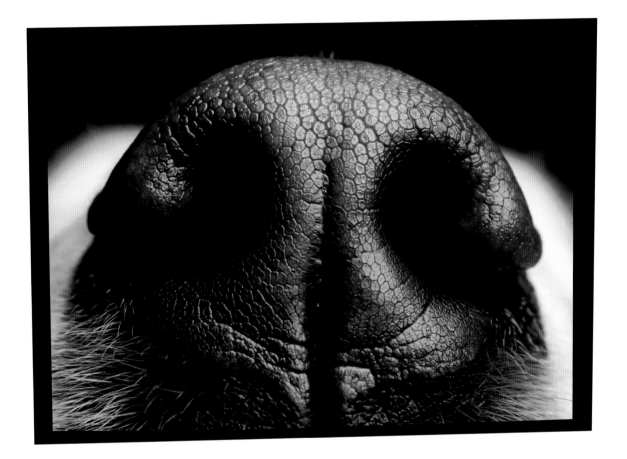

Turn and see!

DOG

A dog has a powerful sniffer! Some people think a dog can pick up the scent of a person's feelings.

Who sniffs with this nose?

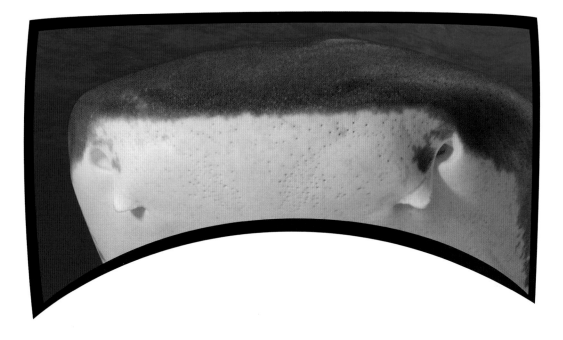

Turn and see!

SHARK

A shark's nose catches scents of a meal from miles away.

Who sniffs with this nose?

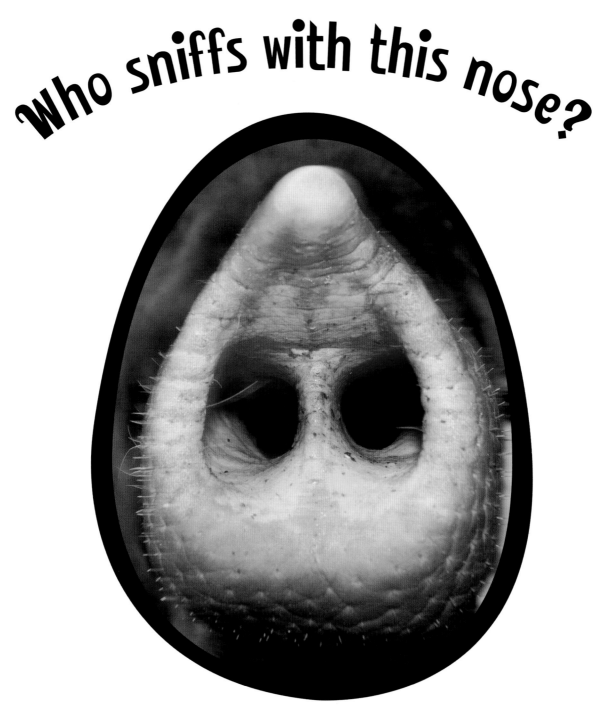

Turn and see!

ELEPHANT

An elephant's long trunk can grab things and squirt water.

Who sniffs with this nose?

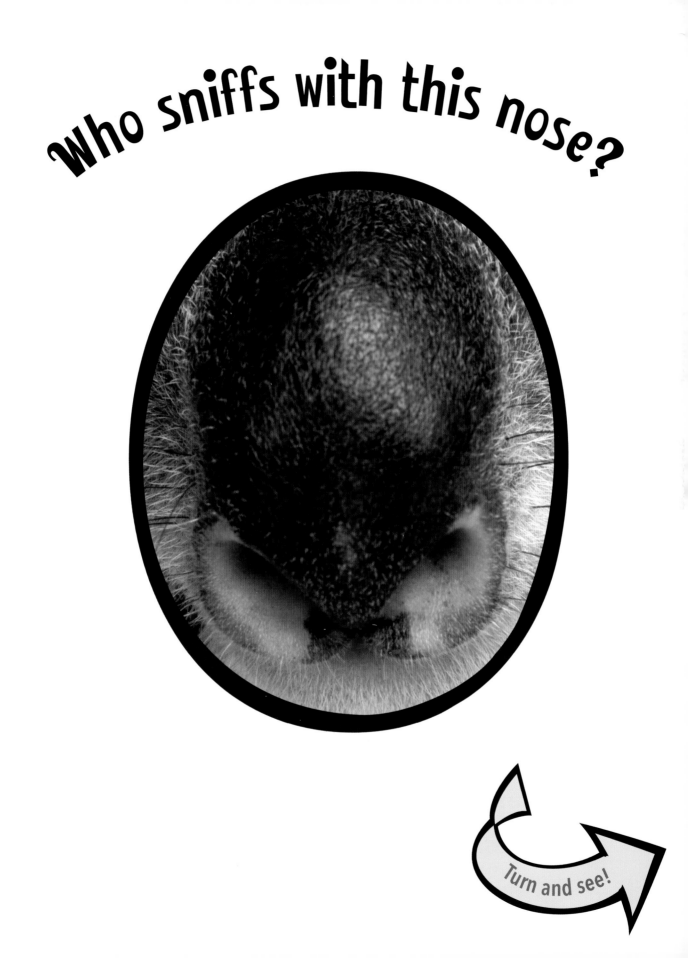

Turn and see!

KOALA

A big black nose smells leaves and can tell which ones are safe to eat.

Who sniffs with this nose?

Turn and see!

AARDVARK

Swinging its nose from side to side, an aardvark picks up the scent of its next meal.

Turn and see!

RABBIT

Twitch, twitch!
A rabbit's nose gathers
smells in the grass.

Who sniffs with this nose?

Turn and see!

ALLIGATOR

An alligator hides underwater but keeps its snout above water to breathe.

Who sniffs with this nose?

Turn and see!

MANDRILL

This beautiful, colorful nose
helps attract a mate.

Who sniffs with this nose?

Turn and see!

CAMEL

This desert animal can close its nostrils so sand doesn't blow into its nose.

Who sniffs with this nose?

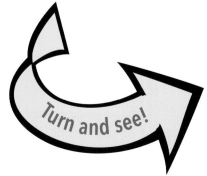
Turn and see!

PIG

A pink snout roots for food in the dirt.

Who sniffs with this nose?

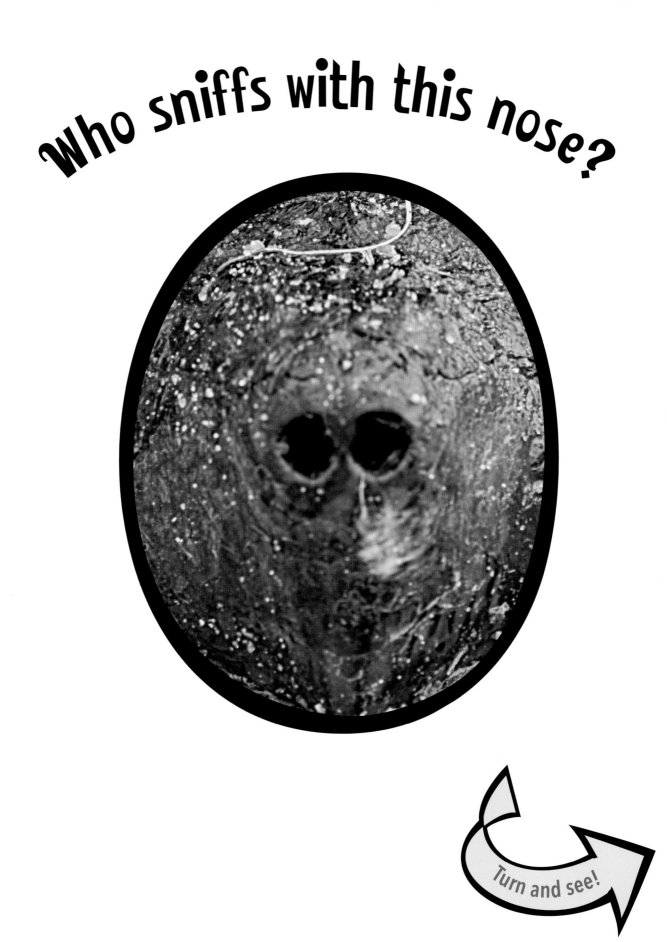

Turn and see!

SNAPPING TURTLE

This leathery nose bumps into things to smell them.

Who sniffs with this nose?

Turn and see!

SEAL

A seal's nostrils shut tight to keep out water.

Who sniffs with this nose?

Turn and see!

STAR-NOSED MOLE

An unusual nose has 22 tentacles to help this mole find food.

Who sniffs with this nose?

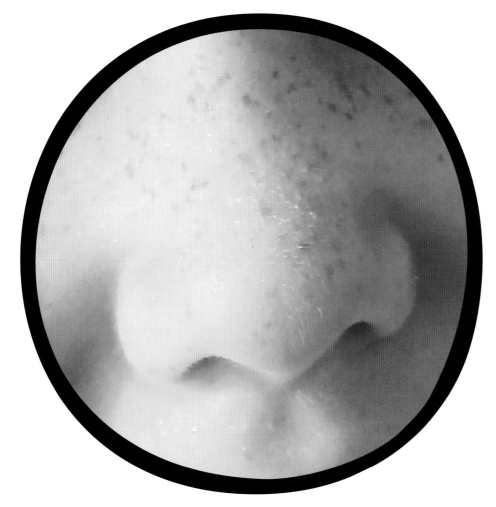

Turn and see!

HUMAN

A child's nose smells the sweet scent of watermelon!

Long or short, noses help animals smell. They pick up the scent of food, sometimes from miles away. Noses are amazing!

Pebble Sprout is published by Pebble, an imprint of Capstone.
1710 Roe Crest Drive
North Mankato, Minnesota 56003
www.capstonepub.com

Library of Congress Cataloging-in-Publication Data is available on the Library of Congress website.
ISBN 978-1-9771-2533-0 (library binding)
ISBN 978-1-9771-2543-9 (eBook PDF)
Summary: Sniff! This photo-guessing game challenges kids to guess whose nose appears in each image. The sniffling and snort-worthy answers may be surprising!

Editor: Shelly Lyons
Designer: Bobbie Nuytten
Media Researcher: Jo Miller
Production Specialist: Katy LaVigne

Image Credits
Getty Images: wendy salisbury photography, 11, 12; Shutterstock: Abdulmajeed Al Juhani, 20, Africa Studio, 3, 4, Agnieszka Bacal, 27, 28, BlueBarronPhoto, 15, D.Cz., 7, Donovan van Staden, 8, Dubova, 29, 30, Eric Isselee, 9, J.R. Sosky, 26, Kevin Collison, 23, Kurit afshen, 17, Laborant, 19, Matt9122, 5, MyImages - Micha, 25, Nikolay 007, 18, Nneirda, 13, Orhan Cam, 16, Simona Weber, 14, Steve Mann, 21, Tiffany Bryant, Cover, Tony Campbell, 24, wildestanimal, 6, William Kuhl Photographs, 22, Yatra, 10

Design Elements
Capstone; Shutterstock: Artishok, cajoer, Fourleaflover, linear_design, srikorn thamniyom

Printed and bound in China.
3322

Good job! Try all the books in this series!

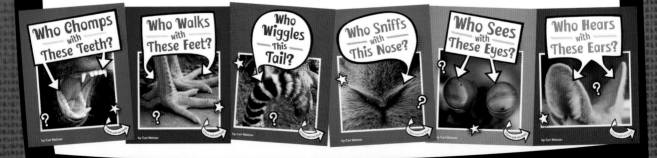